BEARING WITNESS

GENOCIDE AND ETHNIC CLEANSING IN THE MODERN WORLD™

THE DARFUR GENOCIDE

ZOE LOWERY and JANEY LEVY

ROSEN PUBLISHING

NEW YORK

Published in 2017 by The Rosen Publishing Group, Inc.
29 East 21st Street, New York, NY 10010

Library of Congress Cataloging-in-Publication Data

Names: Lowery, Zoe, author. | Levy, Janey, author.
Title: The Darfur genocide / Zoe Lowery and Janey Levy.
Other titles: Bearing witness (Rosen Publishing Group)
Description: New York : Rosen Publishing, 2016. | Series: Bearing witness | Includes bibliographical references and index.
Identifiers: LCCN 2015050305 | ISBN 9781499463064 (library bound)
Subjects: LCSH: Genocide—Sudan--Darfur—Juvenile literature. | Ethnic conflict—Sudan—Darfur—History—20th century—Juvenile literature. | Sudan—History—Darfur Conflict, 2003—Atrocities—Juvenile literature. | Darfur (Sudan)—Ethnic relations—History—20th century—Juvenile literature.
Classification: LCC DT159.6.D27 L69 2016 | DDC 962.7043--dc23
LC record available at http://lccn.loc.gov/2015050305

Manufactured in China

CONTENTS

INTRODUCTION

The term "genocide" is one that is sometimes heard in school during history class or in the news. But what does genocide really mean? Formally, it is stated as the methodical effort to annihilate a certain group of people, especially because of their race, ethnic origin, or faith. Sometimes it has a wider definition to refer to any deliberate government killing of a distinctive group of people for any number of reasons.

The word originates from a blend of the word *genos*, which is Greek for "race," "tribe," or "nation," with *-cide*, which is Latin for "killing." So the root of "genocide" precisely means killing a race, tribe, or nation. A lawyer from Poland, Dr. Raphael Lemkin, first used the word in 1944 in his book about Germany's Nazi strategies and the areas it overpowered during the Second World War.

Unfortunately, genocide has been in practice since as early as 416 BCE, based on recorded history, when Athens, Greece, assaulted Melos and carried out genocide against the islanders there. The 1209 Albigensian Crusade is sometimes referred to as the first "modern" genocide. (In this case, the term "modern" means "not ancient," an event that occurred within the last several hundred years, as opposed to thousands of years in the past.) A holy war against enemies of the faith, known as a crusade, was declared by the leader of the Catholic Church, the pope. Anyone who disputed the instructions of the Catholic Church was labeled as an enemy of the faith. Christians who had varying faiths were assaulted and murdered by Catholic soldiers.

Throughout the twentieth century, many genocides ensued. In 1915, Turkey devastated its Armenian citizens. During the Holocaust of World War II, Nazi Germany's Adolf Hitler orchestrated the killing of six million Jews, along with millions of other minorities. The Holocaust might be the twentieth century's most infamous genocide. As the twentieth century came to a close, the Rwandan genocide resulted in the deaths of eight hundred thousand Rwandan people.

As the twenty-first century began, genocide in Sudan's Darfur area added still another item to this dreadful list. In February 2002, Africans in Darfur initiated a revolt against the

In Scotland, survivors of the Darfur genocide reenact the Janjaweed militia's and Sudanese army's damage to their homes.

Arab-controlled government of Sudan. Soldiers for the government took up arms against the uprising with the support of militias from traveling Arab tribes armed by the government. These militias were called Janjaweed, or devils on horseback. The goal of the government and the Janjaweed was to remove all Africans from Darfur. More than two million Africans had no choice but to leave their homes, and up to five hundred thousand Africans may have died in the process. The horrors of the Darfur genocide have been referred to as the early twenty-first century's cruelest humanitarian disaster.

CHAPTER 1

GENOCIDE THROUGH THE YEARS

The man who would go on to devise the very word "genocide," Dr. Raphael Lemkin, was born in 1900 or 1901 in Poland. As a young man he achieved his a law degree in 1926, and went on to work as an attorney for the Polish government. In 1939, Germany invaded Poland in 1939, and Lemkin fought with the resistance. He went on to escape to Sweden, and from there on to the United States, in 1941. Lemkin's career was primarily spent writing about genocide and in an effort to persuade the nations of the world that international law should make genocide a crime.

Dr. Raphael Lemkin became the driving force behind attaining international recognition of genocide as a war crime.

Propelled by the horrors of the 1915 Armenian genocide and the Iraqi government's 1933 massacre of Iraqi Christians, Lemkin launched an international campaign to outlaw such atrocities. At a 1933 conference on international law held in Madrid, Spain, Lemkin urged that these "acts of barbarity" be condemned as crimes against humanity. He was unsuccessful, but he refused to abandon his campaign. By 1944, when he published his most famous book, *Axis Rule in Occupied Europe*, he had created a special term for these barbarous acts—genocide. Genocide was recognized as a war crime at the Nuremberg Trials (1945–1949) following World War II.

Lemkin was not satisfied with having genocide recognized only as a war crime, however. He also wanted it acknowledged as a crime when committed in peacetime. In 1948, he finally succeeded in convincing the United Nations to make genocide a crime under international law. This meant the international community could punish those who committed genocide no matter when they carried it out.

THE CRIME OF GENOCIDE

In December 1948, the United Nations approved a convention, or agreement, on genocide. The Convention on the Prevention and Punishment of the Crime of Genocide went into effect in January 1951. It made genocide a crime under international law and defined it this way (as quoted by the website for the UN Office of the High Commissioner for Human Rights):

> In the present Convention, genocide means any of the following acts committed with intent to destroy, in

whole or in part, a national, ethnical, racial or religious group, as such:

(a) Killing members of the group;
(b) Causing serious bodily or mental harm to members of the group;
(c) Deliberately inflicting on the group conditions of life calculated to bring about its physical destruction in whole or in part;
(d) Imposing measures intended to prevent births within the group;
(e) Forcibly transferring children of the group to another group.

GENOCIDE THROUGH THE SECOND WORLD WAR

Genocide has probably been practiced since before there was written history. One of the earliest recorded genocides occurred in 416 BCE during the Second Peloponnesian War. The war, fought between the ancient Greek cities of Athens and Sparta, takes its name from the region where it occurred—the southern Greek peninsula known as the Peloponnesus. The island of Melos, once a Spartan colony, tried to remain neutral during the war. However, Athens demanded that Melos submit to Athenian rule and pay tribute money. When the people of Melos refused, the Athenians attacked the island, killed all the men, made slaves of the women and children, and gave the island to Athenian settlers.

Épisode de la guerre des Albigeois (1). — Bas-relief de l'église de Saint-Nazaire, à Carcassonne. — D'après le plâtre conservé au Musée des Thermes et de l'hôtel de Cluny.

A nineteenth-century engraving depicting images from the 1209 Albigensian Crusade

The 1209 Albigensian Crusade pitted Christian against Christian. Southern France was home to a group of people whose version of Christianity was contrary to official Catholic teachings and thus considered heresy. After failing to destroy the heresy through peaceful means, the pope called a crusade against the heretics. Thousands of soldiers from northern Europe descended on southern France. They destroyed cities and crops and exterminated thousands of people. In one town, for example, crusaders killed 15,000 men, women, and children.

In 1913, a coup in Turkey swept a trio of dictators into power. They wanted to build an empire by expanding east, a path that would take them through the homeland of about two million Armenians. Islamic extremists in Turkey decided the best way to achieve their dream of empire was to eliminate the Christian Armenians blocking their way. By 1918, up to 1.5 million Armenians had been killed and the rest driven away. Turks quickly took over the homes and villages once occupied by Armenians.

In 1933, Christian Assyrians in Muslim Iraq suffered a similar fate. Many of the Assyrians had been forced into refugee camps during conflicts from 1914 to 1923. In 1933, the Iraqi government told them they must either relocate to tiny villages scattered among the hostile Muslim population or leave the country. When several hundred Assyrians tried to leave, Iraqi border troops attacked and killed them. The troops then executed unarmed Assyrians in surrounding villages while the Iraqi government did nothing. In the end, more than 3,000 Assyrians were killed.

For many people, the word "genocide" first brings to mind the Holocaust of World War II. Under Adolf Hitler, Germany's Nazi rulers systematically murdered millions of people they considered inferior in some way. The Nazis focused especially on Jews. Their goal was to kill every Jewish man, woman, and child under German rule. It was the religious aspect of the persecution, combined with the fact that many victims' bodies were burned, that led to the use of the term "Holocaust." The word is a religious term that means "a burnt sacrificial offering." In addition to Jews,

Nazis targeted other groups, including Polish people and Roma, or Gypsies. By the time the war ended, the Nazis had murdered perhaps eleven million people, including about six million Jews.

GENOCIDE ON TRIAL

The International Criminal Court (ICC) was created to try individuals accused of genocide, war crimes, and crimes against humanity. Its focus on individuals distinguishes it from the International Court of Justice, which handles disputes between countries. The ICC was established in 1998 at a conference of nations held in Rome, Italy. It came into being in 2002, after sixty countries had approved the agreement establishing the court. Its headquarters are in The Hague, the Netherlands. In 2007, the court announced charges stemming from the Darfur atrocities.

POST–SECOND WORLD WAR GENOCIDE

The 1945–1949 Nuremberg Trials established genocide as a war crime. The 1948 Convention on the Prevention and Punishment of the Crime of Genocide made it an international crime regardless of whether it occurred during wartime or peacetime. Seemingly, the world had been put on notice that the community of nations would no longer tolerate genocide. In spite of this, the second half of the twentieth century saw numerous instances of genocide.

Piles of skulls were uncovered; evidence of the horrors during the Khmer Rouge's brutal Cambodian genocide.

From 1975 to 1979, Pol Pot and the communist Khmer Rouge ruled the Southeast Asian nation of Cambodia. Their radical goal was to create a pure, classless peasant society. The government expelled all foreigners and forced Cambodians living in cities to move to the countryside. They banned all religions and persecuted ethnic and religious minorities such as the Vietnamese, Chinese, Muslims, and Buddhist monks. No one knows for sure how many people were executed or died from disease, starvation, and overwork. Estimates range from one million to more than three million.

Between 1981 and 1983, the Guatemalan government carried out what is sometimes called the Silent Holocaust against the nation's Mayan Indians. Over the course of a civil war that lasted from 1962 to 1996, more than 200,000 people were killed or disappeared. About 83 percent were Maya. The attacks on the Maya were particularly intense between 1981 and 1983. The government claimed the Maya were aiding rebel forces. However, many victims were children, making it clear the government's real purpose was to destroy the Maya. Soldiers tortured and killed Maya and destroyed villages and crops.

The Republic of Bosnia and Herzegovina, once part of the southeast European nation of Yugoslavia, became independent in 1992. Almost immediately, the government began a campaign of genocide against the nation's Muslims and Croats (people from the neighboring country of Croatia). Thousands of Muslim and Croat civilians were imprisoned, expelled, attacked, tortured, and murdered. Their homes, businesses, and places of worship were destroyed. The genocide finally ended in 1995.

During the same period of the Bosnia and Herzegovina genocide, a swift and savage genocide occurred in the central African nation of Rwanda. Problems had long existed between the country's two major ethnic groups, the Tutsis and the Hutus. In 1994, the president, a Hutu, died when his plane was shot down. Within hours, violence erupted. By the time the violence ended about 100 days later, around 800,000 people had been killed. Most of the dead were Tutsis. Most of the killers were Hutus.

CHAPTER 2

SUDAN'S SORDID STORY OF GENOCIDE

Before South Sudan became independent in 2011, the Republic of Sudan was Africa's largest country. At about 976,500 square miles (2,529,123 sq km), Sudan at that time was made up of nine states, including Darfur. The country differs quite a bit between its north and south. The northern part of Sudan encompasses the majority of Sudan's people and cities. Here the bulk of people think of themselves as "Arab" because they descended from earlier Arab immigrants or Africans who embraced the language and ethnicity of the Arabs. Others in the

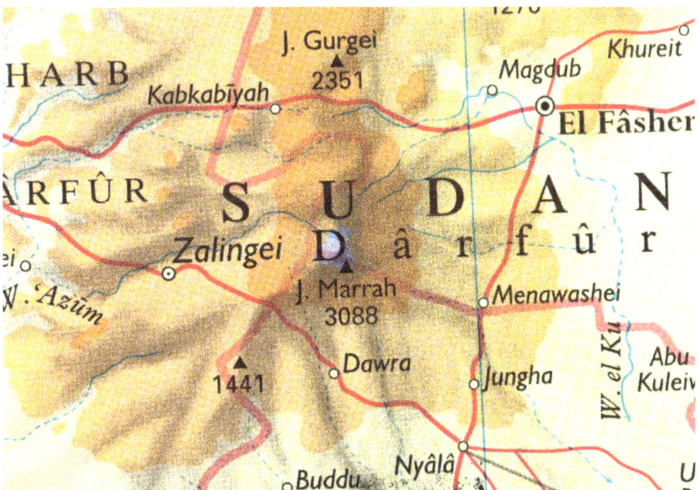

Sudan is one of the largest countries in Africa, with most of its population residing in the northern areas.

north are regarded as "African." Whether they are Arab or African, they are all Muslim. Sudan's southern area is typically rural and has far fewer people than the north. Southern people are thought of as "African," most of whom follow African religious traditions or practice Christianity.

Darfur is in western Sudan. The name "Darfur" means "home of the Fur." *Dar* is the Arabic word for "home." The Fur are the region's dominant ethnic group. The other principal ethnic groups are the Zaghawa and Masalit. Arabs arrived in Darfur between the fourteenth and eighteenth centuries. So much intermarriage between Arabs and native ethnic groups occurred over the centuries that there is now little physical difference between "Arabs" and "Africans." As in northern Sudan, both "Arabs" and "Africans" are Muslim.

Sudan has been independent since 1956. However, the journey that led to the genocide in Darfur began in the late 1800s. It's a complicated tale that involves conquest; internal politics; social, ethnic, racial, and regional tensions; religious extremism; drought, famine, and desertification; civil wars; and the political ambitions of other countries.

SUDANESE POLITICS

In 1898, Britain and Egypt took joint control over Sudan. This didn't include Darfur, which was an independent territory ruled by a sultan. Egypt administered northern Sudan, and Britain administered the south. The arrangement exaggerated existing differences between the two regions. Egypt encouraged Islamic values in the Arabic-speaking north. Britain promoted Christianity in the south and encouraged the use of English. In 1916, Britain added Darfur to the territory it controlled.

After World War II ended in 1945, Britain and Egypt began preparing Sudan for independence. They united Sudan's various regions. The northern city of Khartoum became the capital, and wealthy northern Arabs from around the Nile River received control of the government. Darfur and southern Sudan were excluded from any real power.

Sudan received independence in 1956. However, establishing a permanent government seemed impossible, and the country endured prolonged instability. In 1958, General Ibrahim Abboud led an army coup of the government. Abboud's government lasted only until 1964, when it was overthrown and replaced by a civilian government. Then in 1969, the army again seized control and made Colonel Jaafar Nimeiri the country's leader. Nimeiri's government lasted sixteen years. After a brief period of civilian government, General Omar Hassan Ahmed al-Bashir came

General Ibrahim Abboud (pictured around 1961 in New York City) lead a coup against the Sudanese government in 1956.

to power in a 1989 coup organized by the extremist National Islamic Front (NIF). Darfur, remote from Khartoum and having no valuable resources, suffered neglect from all these governments.

SEEKING A STATE OF ISLAM

Ever since Sudan's independence, extremists zealously pursued a policy of Arabization and Islamization. The result for Sudan's people has been suffering on a massive scale. However, it's important to remember that the extremists' beliefs don't represent all of Sudan's Arabs and Muslims. Tens of thousands of the radicals' victims have been Muslims. Many of Sudan's Arabs have actively opposed the extremists' policies.

Efforts to Islamize southern Sudan began under General Ibrahim Abboud in 1958. In 1964, the radical Muslim Brotherhood formed. Its goal was to create an Islamic state. Islamists gained government positions in the 1970s, and their influence spread. In 1983, Khartoum approved the "September laws," which imposed strict Islamic law on all Sudan. The early 1980s also saw the formation of a supremacist group called the Arab Gathering, or Arab Alliance. In addition, the NIF—the Muslim Brotherhood's political party—became a powerful force in the government. The NIF wanted to make Sudan a key center of the radical Islamic world. Under its influence, Sudan hosted meetings of terrorists and became the home of Osama bin Laden from 1991 to 1996. Most Arab governments shunned the extremist Sudan.

THE ROLE OF CLIMATE

Camel herders in northern Sudan depend on rainfall, and their ways of life were severely disrupted after several natural disasters.

Climate has played a major role in Darfur's settlement patterns and cultural development. The south, which receives 32 to 55 inches (81 to 140 centimeters) of rain annually, is home to farmers and cattle-herding nomads. Camel-herding nomads wander the far north, which receives only about 4 inches (10 cm) of rain annually. Other parts of the north, which may receive up to 32 inches of rain, have farms and industry. Northern nomads moved south to graze their camels in farmland during the dry season. They bought grain from farmers and carried the farmers' goods to distant markets. A series of natural disasters altered these traditional rhythms of life.

The natural disasters that plagued Sudan throughout the twentieth century had particularly devastating effects in Darfur. Drought, water shortages, crop destruction by locusts, famine, and disease were recurring problems. In *Darfur's Sorrow: A History of Destruction and Genocide*, M. W. Daly reports that up to 25 percent of the Fur died in a 1926 disease outbreak. Daly also estimates that more than one hundred thousand Darfurians died during drought and famine in 1984 and 1985. In addition, desertification spread in the far north.

The continuing drought and desertification affected

northern nomads the most. People and animals were forced to permanently move south in search of water and grazing land. This migration placed environmental stress on lands already occupied by farmers. It also led to competition for increasingly limited resources and fueled tension between ethnic groups.

CIVIL WAR

In 1958, Abboud's campaign of Islamization and Arabization led to civil war. Southern rebels formed a guerrilla army called Anya-Nya, which means "snake poison." The war finally ended in 1972, when Khartoum and Anya-Nya signed a peace treaty.

In 1983, Khartoum broke the treaty, and civil war erupted again. The discovery of oil in southern Sudan gave Khartoum even more reason to seek control of the region. The Sudan People's Liberation Movement (SPLM) and the Sudan People's Liberation Army (SPLA), led by John Garang, headed the south's rebellion.

In response, Khartoum developed tactics it would continue to use in its quest to Islamicize and Arabize the entire country. The government armed and trained ethnic militias to fight the rebels and civilians who supported them. It also used rebel armies from other countries. In addition, Khartoum—in violation of international law—used starvation as a weapon of war by preventing aid workers from delivering food to people in the south. According to Don Cheadle and John Prendergast in *Not on Our Watch*, more than five hundred thousand people starved to death in 1992 and 1993.

Under pressure from the United States and other countries, peace talks began in 2001. The two sides finally signed the Comprehensive Peace Agreement (CPA) in 2005. It called for the north and south to share power for six years, at which time the south would vote on self-determination. It also stated Islamic law would not be imposed on the south. Unfortunately, the CPA began to fall apart in late 2007. The SPLM complained that Khartoum was not fulfilling the agreement and withdrew from the joint government.

REFUGEES

Civil wars produce refugees and internally displaced persons (IDPs). Refugees are people who have had to flee their home and country to escape conflict or persecution. Usually they go to neighboring countries. IDPs are just like refugees except they haven't left their country. They have simply moved internally, within their country, to an area that is far from the fighting. About six hundred thousand refugees fled the civil war between Khartoum and the SPLA. The war also drove an estimated four million people from their homes.

Habillah, Darfur, is filled with thousands of internally displaced persons (IDPs), like this woman and her child.

DIFFICULTIES IN LIBYA, CHAD, AND DARFUR

Government troops from the neighboring country of Chad pursued the rebels into Darfur. Libya, to the northwest, saw an opportunity to further its pursuit of empire. It provided weapons to Darfur's Zaghawa and Arab nomads. It also fueled Darfur's ethnic tensions with propaganda about how "Africans" had denied "Arabs" their rights. Concerned the propaganda might lead to violence, the Fur organized militias for self-protection. Chad's government supplied arms to them. In 1987, war erupted between Fur militias and Arab Janjaweed. It ended in 1989, but Janjaweed attacks on "African" villages continued.

Darfur's situation worsened after the NIF came to power in 1989. Libya agreed to provide military aid to the NIF in its civil war with southern Sudan. In exchange, the NIF allowed Libya to use Darfur as a base from which to build its empire. Fighting across Darfur's border with Chad intensified. Chadians destroyed Fur and Zaghawa villages.

BOYS ON THE RUN

The second civil war between Khartoum and southern Sudan produced a generation of orphans and boys separated from their families. Known as the Lost Boys, they were forced to flee to avoid slavery, death, or being forced to fight for Khartoum. They walked hundreds of miles to reach refugee camps in Ethiopia. Ten thousand reached the camps, but thousands of others had died on the journey. Then the Ethiopian government was overthrown in 1991, and the boys had to flee again. Sixteen thousand boys—and some girls—reached Kakuma refugee camp in Kenya. Others went to other Kenyan camps. In 2000, the U.S. government began to bring some of the Lost Boys to America.

THE *BLACK BOOK*

In May 2000, the so-called *Black Book* was published. The unknown authors presented facts demonstrating that Khartoum's neglect of Darfur and other regions remote from the capital was intentional. The book's goal was to move the Sudanese people to take action that would bring about profound change in Sudan. It had a significant effect in Darfur. The book helped unite Darfurians from different backgrounds and ethnic groups who wanted to force changes that would aid Darfur. In 2001, a group of leaders formed the Justice and Equality Movement (JEM). JEM called for radical constitutional reform and increased power for neglected regions.

Also in 2001, Fur and Zaghawa rebel leaders formed the Darfur Liberation Front (DLF) to fight the NIF and Janjaweed. The Masalit joined the DLF later that year. In February 2002, the DLF launched its first battle. It attacked and destroyed a government post. Organized rebellion had begun. Khartoum responded with a massive genocide campaign.

CHAPTER 3

SLAUGHTER IN DARFUR

After the February 2002 DLF attack on the government post, Fur leaders presented a list of Janjaweed atrocities to the government. Khartoum offered a few artificial attempts to discuss peace with the rebels. In reality they were trying to gain more time to organize their plans for Darfur. Meanwhile, Janjaweed attacks continued.

In October 2002, the DLF elected leaders. They included representatives of the Fur, Zaghawa, and Masalit tribes, as well as several Arabs. The DLF slowly transformed into the Sudan Liberation Movement (SLM) and the Sudan Liberation Army (SLA). In February

In September 2002, Islamist militiamen prepared to confront the Sudanese People's Liberation Army (SPLA).

2003, the SLA attacked a government garrison and killed two hundred soldiers. The following month, the SLM/SLA issued a manifesto spelling out its goals. It called for a secular state and self-determination for Darfur. It condemned oppression and urged Darfur's Arabs to join the SLM/SLA in bringing about a "New Sudan."

For the next several months, the SLA and JEM enjoyed a series of victories against the government and Janjaweed. However, the situation soon began to change. At first, the government and Janjaweed had focused most of their attacks on rebel camps. In mid-2003, they began to concentrate their attacks on civilians. The genocide had begun.

GOVERNMENT SCHEME

The SLA and JEM experienced so many victories against government soldiers in early 2003 because they fought a guerrilla-style war. The regular Sudanese army could not successfully combat this type of fighting. The government recognized that it needed to employ a different approach to defeat the rebels. Khartoum declared a state of emergency and arrested hundreds of rebel supporters. It also created a plan to use the Janjaweed to fight the rebels. The army would provide assistance, but the Janjaweed would do the major fighting. This would allow the government to claim the fighting in Darfur was just the usual tribal conflict and the government was not responsible for it. At the same time, it would allow Khartoum to accomplish its goal: driving all "Africans" out of Darfur. The government knew what the results of using the Janjaweed would be. They had used similar militias during the civil war with the south and had seen what happened there.

The government recruited for the Janjaweed among the Arab tribes and paid Arab sheikhs for their support, offering cash and promising future development to improve the tribes' lives. However, in spite of the government's efforts, some Arab tribes refused to take part in the genocide.

Any non-Arabs who tried to join the Janjaweed were rejected. However, any Arabs at all—including criminals—were accepted. In fact, the government actively recruited criminals for the Janjaweed. Khartoum also took steps to improve the Janjaweed's fighting abilities. It provided weapons, communications equipment, military advisers, and training.

ATROCITIES

Attacks on civilians by the Janjaweed and government soldiers increased even as fighting with the rebels declined. Soldiers and the Janjaweed commonly worked together. Soldiers bombed a village or town, then the Janjaweed moved in. After the Janjaweed were finished, soldiers killed or captured anyone left alive. There's evidence soldiers used chemical weapons in their attacks.

The Janjaweed tortured, shot, and stabbed civilians. They shouted racial slurs and called their victims "slaves." They shouted claims that the land belonged to "Arabs," not to "Africans." The Janjaweed sometimes lined up men and boys and shot them in the back of the head. They tossed children into burning houses. They chained schoolchildren together and burned them alive. Women and girls were raped, often more than once. Some rape victims were killed, some were not. For the women and girls of Darfur, rape was not only a horrific experience but also a source of great shame. In order to make their suffering worse, the Janjaweed sometimes branded rape victims so that everyone who saw them would know what had happened to them.

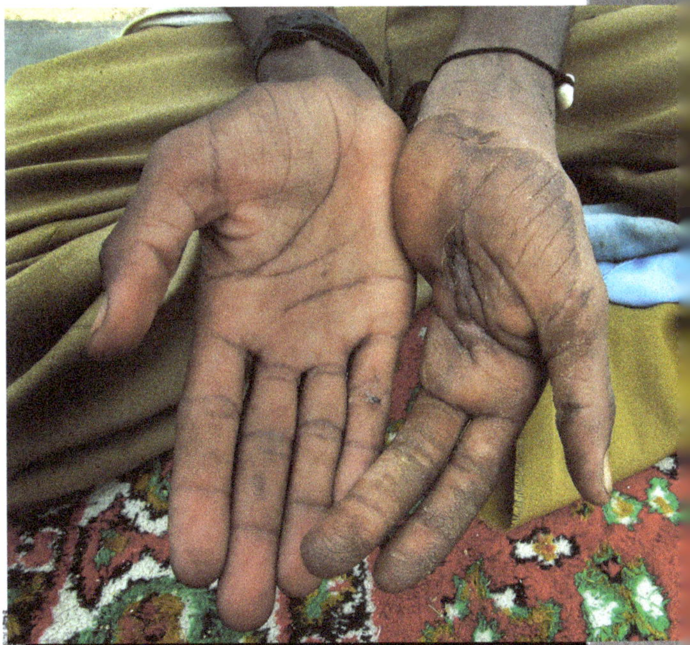

A victim of the Janjaweed's torture reveals his scars and missing fingers from a 2004 attack on his village.

Villagers who managed to escape or survive Janjaweed attacks lost everything. The Janjaweed took anything of value in the villages and towns. They destroyed clinics, schools, mosques, and entire villages. They even tore apart copies of the Quran, the Muslims' holy book. They stole or destroyed food and animals. They poisoned the water by throwing dead bodies into wells. They wanted to leave nothing for survivors to return to. After they had finished, Arabs sometimes settled on the land and gave the place a new name in Arabic.

Why did local officials do nothing to stop the genocide? Khartoum had issued orders not to interfere with the Janjaweed. In fact, Khartoum ordered local officials to give the Janjaweed whatever they needed. In addition, many police and government officials simply left Darfur. Civilians had no protection except what the SLA and JEM could offer.

When word of what was happening in Darfur finally reached the outside world, Khartoum at first simply denied it. The government claimed the stories were lies and propaganda that reflected the Western world's bias against Arabs and Islam. Finally, Khartoum agreed to cooperate with aid agencies trying to get food and other supplies to refugees and IDPs. Then the government delayed the delivery of food and supplies. Khartoum also tried to deceive the world into believing it was taking action to halt the genocide in Darfur. It arranged fake handovers of Janjaweed weapons for reporters to witness. It took convicts from prison, proclaimed they were Janjaweed, and executed them. All the while, the genocide continued.

Since Khartoum kept reporters and aid workers out of Darfur, it was hard to know how many refugees and IDPs there were. Since the Janjaweed threw bodies down wells, burned them, or buried them in mass graves, it was hard to know how many had been killed. It's estimated that up to five hundred thousand were killed. Chad sheltered two hundred thousand or more refugees. Inside Darfur, there were approximately two million IDPs.

RELIEF WORKERS ATTACKED

Even aid workers, whose only goal was to help refugees and IDPs, were not safe in Darfur. Fighting sometimes forced them to leave areas where their help was needed. Their bases were attacked. Their vehicles were attacked or stolen to prevent them from reaching people who needed aid. In 2006, more than one hudred vehicles belonging to aid workers were stolen. Aid supplies were also stolen. Even workers themselves were attacked. At least thirteen aid workers were killed in 2006.

CEASE-FIRES AND OTHER STEPS TOWARD PEACE

Efforts were made to end the atrocities. In 2003, the president of Chad got both sides to agree to a forty-five-day cease-fire so that aid could be delivered to refugees and IDPs. Unfortunately, neither side honored the cease-fire.

New peace talks were held in 2004. This time the African Union (AU)—a group of African nations that promotes cooperation and provides aid to member nations—also took part. Another cease-fire was reached. It called for the government to disarm the Janjaweed and provide aid agencies with full access to refugees and IDPs. It also established a committee to monitor the cease-fire. In addition, it called for AU peacekeepers in Darfur. However, the peacekeepers were only authorized to protect the cease-fire monitoring committee. They had no authority to protect the people of Darfur. Just as happened with the 2003 cease-fire, neither side honored this temporary peace agreement.

Attempts to reach a permanent peace deal continued in 2005. The efforts were complicated by the fact that the rebels found it increasingly difficult to act in a unified fashion, with a single voice. Different groups had different ideas, and the SLA broke into separate units. In January 2006, the AU called for the United Nations to take over its role in Darfur. Khartoum didn't want this. The government feared it would lose control and never regain it. So Khartoum finally signed the Darfur Peace Agreement (DPA). Unlike the earlier agreements, the DPA was not simply a cease-fire. It established a framework for peace and security, required Khartoum to disarm the Janjaweed, and called for constitutional changes affecting the entire country. Unfortunately, only one unit of the divided SLA signed the agreement. In the end, the DPA proved no more effective at halting the violence than the earlier agreements. Fighting and the suffering of Darfur's people continued.

Sudanese foreign minister Lam Akol gives a press conference in 2006, encouraging more groups to sign the Darfur Peace Agreement.

CHAPTER 4

PREDATOR AND PREY

Khartoum did everything it could to make sure the atrocities in Darfur were not revealed to the rest of the world. Relief workers and reporters were not allowed in. Anyone who broadcast material about the actions or discussed it with foreigners was punished. Relief workers and reporters could not be stopped from getting to the evacuees who poured into Chad. Soon the rest of the world was learning about Darfur's terrors.

Soldiers believed to belong to the Janjaweed militia pause at a Mistiria market in north Darfur.

STORIES FROM THE SURVIVORS

In *Darfur: A Short History of a Long War*, Julie Flint and Alex de Waal recount a story of a 2004 Janjaweed attack told by a young man who survived. The young man told how the Janjaweed executed a group of the village's young men. The Janjaweed cut the throat of the young man's mother. They raped and killed his oldest sister. They killed his brother and father. They threw all the bodies in the well. The young man was the only member of his family to survive. He escaped by hiding under a dead mule.

Flint and de Waal also report another man's story about two attacks his village suffered in 2003. The Janjaweed came alone the first time. They killed forty-two men. They killed sixteen people attending a funeral in the mosque. They burned eighty of the village's three hundred huts. They stole more than three thousand cows, as well as goats, sheep, horses, and donkeys. A few weeks later, the Janjaweed returned. This time soldiers came with them. The soldiers stood around the village and watched while the Janjaweed killed eighty people, including women and children.

In *Not on Our Watch*, Don Cheadle and John Prendergast relate the story of a woman who escaped a Janjaweed attack on her village. The Janjaweed killed her mother, husband, and five children. The woman walked for seven nights to reach a refugee camp. During the day, she hid under trees and plants so the Janjaweed wouldn't find her.

Cheadle and Prendergast also tell another woman's story. The Janjaweed shot her husband when he walked out of their hut. The woman gathered her four children and ran. She carried two children on her back and two in her arms. Twenty Janjaweed chased her on camels. They snatched one of her sons and threw him into the burning village. Then they grabbed another and shot him.

Brian Steidle recounts a story of an attack by soldiers in *The Devil Came on Horseback*. A young woman carried her one-year-old daughter and three-year-old son as she fled government soldiers. Trying to protect her children from the soldiers' gunfire, the young woman was killed. Both children were wounded. The children were still alive when Steidle encountered them with a group of women and children fleeing the Janjaweed. He doesn't know whether they survived or not.

Steidle also relates a story of an attack on a small IDP camp. The day before the camp's market day, the Janjaweed appeared and camped nearby. On market day, the Janjaweed attacked. They whipped and shot people and stabbed one man. Altogether, they killed ten people and wounded seventeen. They also stole thirty-one boxes of food and almost all the camp's medicine. To make matters worse, the IDPs actually knew their attackers. The Janjaweed were nomads the villagers used to trade with.

LIES?

Brian Steidle served with the 2004 cease-fire monitoring committee in Darfur. He reports that soldiers who attacked villages often justified their actions with stories that were obviously lies. For example, they might falsely claim the reason they attacked a marketplace filled with civilians was because rebels hiding in the marketplace had attacked them first. Soldiers also often falsely claimed the reason they attacked a village was that bandits there had attacked them first. Unfortunately, the cease-fire monitoring committee had no authority to take action. They could only write reports.

The "devils on horseback," or Janjaweed, torched and destroyed villages and tortured innocent citizens.

DEVILS ON HORSEBACK

Who were the Janjaweed? Why were they willing to commit atrocities against civilians? As noted earlier, some were criminals. Khartoum promised them land, livestock, and whatever they could steal. However, the criminals formed only part of the Janjaweed. What motivated the other members?

A long history of resentment and injustice led many Arabs to take up arms. Cattle-herding Arab nomads who settled in the south, with its widely scattered population and open land, received large areas of land over which they could move and graze their cattle. However, camel-herding Arab nomads who settled in the more-crowded north never received land. They felt mistreated in comparison to the cattle-herding nomads. In spite of their resentment, they originally had good relations with the Fur farmers to the south. The farmers welcomed the nomads when they came to graze their camels. The nomads bought grain from the farmers and carried their goods to market.

Drought and desertification destroyed the grazing land of camel-herding nomads. The camels of some groups died. Poverty increased greatly. The Fur farmers, also hurt by drought and desertification, no longer welcomed the nomads. Trying to protect their damaged land from the added strain of grazing camels, the farmers built fences or burned grass to block the nomads' way. The nomads were forced to find other routes to grazing land farther south. Tension rose between nomads and farmers.

Recurring drought drove many of Chad's Arabs to migrate to Darfur. This enlarged Darfur's Arab population and added to the tension between "Arabs" and "Africans." At the same time, sheikhs trying to expand their power recruited Arabs from Chad to join their tribes, further increasing Darfur's Arab population and raising tension.

Meanwhile, Libya and the Arab Gathering spread Arab supremacist propaganda. Driven by desperation and spurred by this propaganda, many Arabs joined the Janjaweed. In *Not on Our Watch*, Cheadle and Prendergast report many young

Arabs felt they had no economic alternative. Janjaweed leaders took advantage of the situation by recruiting in Sudan's poorest areas. They offered about $100—a lot of money to desperately poor people—to anyone who would join. To build larger Janjaweed forces, they also recruited in neighboring countries.

Among the Janjaweed leaders who exploited Arab desperation and poverty was Abd al-Rahman Abdallah Jadallah, the director of Nomad Education in North Darfur. He was in charge of recruitment. Another was Abd al-Rahim Ahmad Muhammad, an army officer who had been sent to prison for abandoning his post. He proclaimed himself Izrael, the Angel of Death. At the top was Musa Hilal, the "captain of all captains" and an Arab Gathering leader. He taught new recruits that civilians from the rebels' tribes were also enemies, and he supervised many attacks on civilians himself.

GOVERNMENT ACTIONS

Musa Hilal received orders directly from Khartoum. The government denied it, but Hilal didn't. The Janjaweed operated with the government's authorization and support. The government head during the genocide in Darfur was General Omar

Janjaweed militia chief Musa Hilal speaks in 2009. He admits to having received orders from Khartoum, but the government denies it.

Hassan Ahmed al-Bashir, who came to power in a 1989 military coup.

After fighting erupted in Darfur in 2002, al-Bashir publicly vowed to use the army, police, and Janjaweed to destroy the rebellion. In this and his other decisions, he was following the extremist National Islamic Front (NIF), the leading power in the government.

National Islamic Front NIF leader Hassan al-Turabi pictured about 1993

The NIF was committed to making Sudan an Islamic state by any means possible. They were even willing to conduct jihad against other Muslims. When the people of Darfur sought government protection against Arab militia attacks in the 1990s, the NIF ignored them. The NIF put Musa Hilal in charge of the Janjaweed and armed and trained them. The NIF instructed local officials in Darfur not to interfere with the Janjaweed but to give them whatever they needed.

The NIF's leader was Hassan al-Turabi. Off and on, al-Turabi held official positions in the government. However, regardless of his official position, al-Turabi was responsible for developing plans and policies for the NIF's Islamic state.

Ali Osman Mohammed Taha's job was to direct implementation of al-Turabi's plans and policies. He held several powerful government positions and finally became al-Bashir's vice president. Hilal considered Ali Osman the Hero of Sudan.

Under the NIF, the government imposed forced starvation on Darfur's IDPs. Such use of starvation as a weapon of war violates international law, but the NIF didn't care. The government found many ways to delay aid and aid workers. Workers had to receive visas to enter the country. Then they had to get travel and fuel permits. Health workers had to fulfill exacting registration requirements. Medicines had to be tested for "safety." Delivery of workers' vehicles was delayed. When the vehicles finally reached Darfur, the government often seized them. When food at last reached the camps, armed men "guarding" the camps took the food for themselves. These "guards" sometimes didn't even allow IDPs to bring in wild food they had gathered. Khartoum clearly meant to achieve its stated goal of removing all "Africans" from Darfur in order to make it "Arab" and "Islamic."

CHAPTER 5

INTERNATIONAL RESPONSE

A private report from the 2003 Arab Gathering's political committee was issued, stressing the need to make sure incidents in Darfur remained undisclosed. The fact that secrecy was of the utmost importance was not lost on Khartoum. It depended on the world's concern with actions in the south keeping their attentions off Darfur. This was true for a while. Other countries were interested in oil options in the south, so they were very enthusiastic for successful peace talks between Khartoum and southern rebels. It's unclear whether they were aware of what was going on in Darfur or if they didn't think it was a concern. As information leaked out, Khartoum was badgered to put an end to it by nations—led by the United States—groups, and individuals.

NEWS SUBDUED

Khartoum took extreme steps to subdue information about the genocide in Darfur. It prohibited Sudanese journalists from reporting the atrocities. Newspapers that published information about Darfur were suppressed. Even reporters who wrote stories about rebel attacks were threatened or arrested.

Khartoum denied visas to foreign reporters or didn't allow them to travel to Darfur. Sudanese who talked to foreign reporters or aid workers were arrested and jailed. Aid workers who were suspected of leaking information might be forced to leave the country. Khartoum shut down Al Jazeera, the world's most watched Arabic-language television station, after it broke the news about the atrocities in Darfur.

In spite of Khartoum's efforts, some aid workers and journalists reached Darfur, and stories about the genocide began to leak out. Reporters and aid workers also learned what was happening from refugees in Chad. Khartoum had no power to block access to the refugees, so it tried to keep more Darfurians from reaching Chad. The government offered the Masalit along the border money to prevent Darfurians from entering Chad. The Masalit refused. In response, the government burned Masalit villages and sent soldiers to patrol the border. Still, refugees reached Chad, and reporters and aid workers crossed the border from Chad into Darfur. Khartoum stepped up its efforts. More Sudanese were arrested on suspicion of passing information to foreigners. The government even posted police outside a hospital to keep reporters from talking to patients injured in Janjaweed attacks. In the end, however, Khartoum couldn't keep the genocide secret.

MEDIA REPORTS FROM AFAR

Foreign journalists' early reports weren't very accurate. Many accounts were written from distant places such as Nairobi, Kenya, or Johannesburg, South Africa, where reporters could get only third-hand information. Eventually, more experienced reporters went directly to Khartoum, Chad, and Darfur. However, it was still a full two years after the first Darfur Liberation Front attack in 2002 before foreign newspapers published detailed articles about the genocide.

Nicholas Kristof (pictured in 2015) began reporting on Darfur in 2004 but soon began to campaign to bring the genocide to the public's attention.

The *New York Times* op-ed writer Nicholas Kristof began reporting on Darfur in March 2004. He initially agreed to do a single story on refugees in Chad after hearing about them from aid workers. Shocked by what he learned when he visited the camps, Kristof began a personal campaign to bring the genocide to public attention and force the U.S. government to take action. Many people have credited Kristof with bringing the story into the open. He won a Pulitzer Prize in 2006 for his columns on Darfur.

About the same time Kristof began writing about Darfur, newspapers in Europe also began to devote more attention to the genocide. *Le Monde* presented detailed accounts to the people of France. In Britain, the *Guardian* led the way in reporting events.

U.S. television networks were slow to cover the genocide and gave little airtime to the story. According to Prevent Genocide International, in June 2005, the major U.S. networks aired fifty times as many stories about musician Michael Jackson as they did about Darfur. They aired twelve times as many stories about actor Tom Cruise.

ATTENTIVENESS AND ACTION

As news about Darfur emerged in 2004, numerous groups and individuals began efforts to raise public awareness and press for government action. A meeting of forty nonprofit organizations in July 2004 led to the formation of the Save Darfur Coalition. The coalition grew to include more than 180 organizations representing 130 million people. It engaged in public education, mobilized citizens to pressure government leaders, ran television ads, and suggested actions people could take.

College students also formed organizations. In 2004, Nate Wright, Martha Heinemann, and Ben Bixby created Students Taking Action Now: Darfur (STAND). STAND worked to increase awareness and raise funds, and the group also campaigned for a political solution to the conflict. Mark Hanis and

REFUGEES AND IDP SURVIVAL

Arabs sheltered some IDPs who reached Arab regions. However, most refugees and IDPs lived in camps. Sometimes the camps were created for them by aid agencies. Sometimes they created the camps themselves. If they were lucky, they got food and supplies from aid agencies. Unfortunately, many Darfurian refugees and IDPs were not lucky. Safety was also a problem in the camps. Women and girls who left the camps to search for food, water, or firewood could be raped or killed by the Janjaweed. The Janjaweed even attacked the camps. At the end of 2004, conditions in the camps were so bad that one United Nations (UN) official estimated ten thousand people were dying in them every month.

Women walk through the Otash camp for internally displaced people in southern Darfur. It was dangerous for women and girls to leave the camp.

Andrew Sniderman organized the Genocide Intervention Fund (GIF) to raise money to support the African Union peacekeeping force. Early in 2005, Wright, Stephanie Nyombayire from GIF, and film student Andrew Karlsruher traveled to the border between Chad and Darfur to make a film about the refugees' plight. Funding was provided by mtvU, part of MTV. Later in 2005, STAND and GIF united to form the Genocide Intervention Network (GI-Net), which conducted fund-raising and public education. It also mobilized high school and college students through more than eight hundred chapters of STAND.

Actor Angelina Jolie is just one of the high-profile celebrities who endeavored to raise awareness about the genocide in Darfur.

Individuals as well as groups sought to raise awareness and promote action. Eric Reeves, a professor of English, began writing about Sudan during the civil war between Khartoum and the south. He later turned his attention to the Darfur genocide. He wrote numerous articles, presented evidence to Congress, and gave lectures around the country. Brian Steidle, who served with the 2004 cease-fire monitoring committee, wrote a book, made a film, and gave numerous lectures. Actor Don Cheadle and former government official John Prendergast traveled in Darfur, wrote a book, and gave lectures.

Cheadle wasn't the only celebrity who took up Darfur's cause. Angelina Jolie is a Goodwill Ambassador for the United Nations High Commissioner for Refugees (UNHCR) as well as a movie star. She visited refugee camps in Chad, met with government officials, and took part in conferences around the world. Actor George Clooney traveled to Sudan and Chad, appeared on *Oprah*, held a press conference with senators Barack Obama and Sam Brownback, and addressed the UN Security Council. Actor Mia Farrow visited Darfur and Chad and wrote numerous op-ed articles. Actor Mira Sorvino addressed Congress about the plight of women in Darfur and helped organize a concert to raise money and awareness. Numerous other celebrities also acted on Darfur's behalf. Some people criticized the celebrities, saying none of their actions actually helped Darfur's people. Others believed celebrity involvement drew more attention to the cause and thus helped raise awareness.

PREVENTING GENOCIDE

Here are some things you can do to help stop genocide wherever it occurs:

- Write to the president urging that the United States act to end genocide.
- Write to Congress.
- Get involved with organizations working to end genocide.
- Attend an event.
- Organize an event.
- Help raise awareness by telling family and friends about genocide.
- Help raise money.

IN PURSUIT OF PEACE

The African Union peacekeeping mission begun in 2004 floundered. It had authority to protect only the monitoring committee, not civilians. It had too few troops and too little money. In 2006, the AU publicly called for the UN to take over peacekeeping in Darfur. Khartoum resisted the idea, refusing to allow UN forces in Sudan. Finally, however, after enormous international pressure, Khartoum agreed to admit a UN peacekeeping force. In summer 2007, the UN authorized a force of twenty-six thousand to work under the direction of the AU alongside the AU force. The UN forces were scheduled to arrive in early 2008.

In early October 2007, a group of world leaders known as "the Elders" visited Sudan to promote peace and urge all parties to attend the new round of peace talks scheduled for the end of October. The group included former U.S. president Jimmy Carter and Desmond Tutu, a South African leader and winner of the 1984 Nobel Peace Prize. Though their mission was to encourage a political solution to the conflict, they were outspoken in their criticism of the government after visiting Darfur. They also urged Western countries to provide strong support for the joint AU-UN peacekeeping force.

Unfortunately, obstacles continued to block peace efforts. In late September 2007, a group of rebels attacked an AU base, killing ten peacekeepers and wounding several more. In response, government soldiers launched revenge attacks on two Darfur towns. When peace talks began in Tripoli, Libya, in late October 2007, only twenty rebels were present. The main rebel leaders refused to attend. One of those leaders announced he would not attend talks until the joint AU-UN peacekeeping force was in place.

Even in 2015, refugees struggled to survive under tough conditions and with limited supplies, such as water, in Darfur refugee camps.

As the search for peace continued, more than two million refugees and IDPs waited for a chance to return to what was left of their homes. They waited in crowded camps under dreadful conditions, with little food, water, and medical care. They waited for the world to care enough to stop the genocide.

In 2014, the Janjaweed, now known in Sudan as Rapid Support Forces, continued to terrorize Darfur, destroying 127 empty villages and attacking some areas more than once in a matter of months. But the majority of people are opposed to their government's genocide and speak out. For example, Sudan Change Now, a movement made up of youth, started a campaign called Not in Our Name to intensify "the voices of Sudanese (from all regions) resisting the current regime," Akshaya Kumar reported for Al Jazeera America.

Peace efforts are slow. South Sudan declared its independence from Sudan in 2011, but there have been more than two hundred attacks since then, according to SaveDarfur.org. In 2014, United Nations peace talks threatened to fall apart completely because of the continuing conflicts in Sudan. And in 2015, Fatou Bensouda, prosecutor of the International Criminal Court (ICC), was outspoken in her opinion that the United Nations Security Council (UNSC) was merely delivering "empty promises," as quoted in the *Sudan Tribune*. "Despite my repeated requests for the Council to take action with respect to Sudan's blatant disregard of its obligations, and in violation of this Council's Resolutions, my appeals continue to be unheeded."

TIMELINE

FOURTEENTH TO EIGHTEENTH CENTURIES Arab nomads arrive in Darfur. Cattle-herding nomads settle in the south, where they receive land. Camel-herding nomads settle in the north. They don't receive land.

1898 Egypt and Britain take joint control of Sudan (not including Darfur). Egypt administers northern Sudan; Britain administers the south.

TWENTIETH CENTURY Drought, desertification, water shortages, crop destruction by locusts, famine, and disease are recurring problems throughout the century. Darfur suffers intensely. Northern Arab nomads suffer the most. Poverty greatly increases among nomads. Over time, nomads move into central and southern Darfur, straining resources.

1916 Britain takes control of Darfur.

1945 Egypt and Britain begin preparing Sudan for independence. They make the northern city of Khartoum the capital and give control of the government to wealthy northern Arabs from around the Nile River.

1956 Sudan becomes independent.

1958 General Ibrahim Abboud seizes control in a coup. He begins a campaign to Islamize southern Sudan.

1962 Civil war in Chad. Chadian rebels and refugees come to Darfur, straining resources. Chadian soldiers follow rebels into Darfur. Chad stirs tensions between "Arabs" and "Africans" in Darfur with propaganda.

1964 Abboud's government is overthrown and replaced by a civilian government. The radical Muslim Brotherhood forms. Its goal is to create an Islamic state.

1969 Colonel Jaafar Nimeiri takes control in a coup. Under him, Islamists are appointed to government positions. Their influence spreads.

1980S Supremacist group called the Arab Gathering, or Arab Alliance, forms. The National Islamic Front (NIF) becomes a powerful force in the government.

1983 Khartoum approves "September laws," which impose strict Islamic law on all Sudan.

1985 Nimeiri's government is overthrown and replaced with a civilian government.

1987–1989 War in Darfur between Fur militias and Arab Janjaweed. Janjaweed attacks continue after war ends.

1989 The NIF organizes a coup that brings General Omar Hassan Ahmed al-Bashir to power. The NIF allows Libya to use Darfur as a base for building its empire. Chad destroys Darfurian villages.

2000 *Black Book* is published. It recounts government neglect of Darfur.

2001 Justice and Equality Movement (JEM) forms in Darfur. Fur, Zaghawa, and Masalit rebel leaders form the Darfur Liberation Front (DLF).

2002 The DLF attacks a government post, starting a civil war between Darfur and the government and Janjaweed forces.

2003 The DLF becomes the Sudan Liberation Movement (SLM) and Sudan Liberation Army (SLA). The government creates plan to use Janjaweed to fight rebels. Janjaweed begin-sto focus attacks on civilians.

2004 Widespread reporting of Darfur genocide. Organizations and individuals began to urge government action to halt the genocide.

2005 The SLA breaks apart into separate units.

2006 The government and one SLA unit sign Darfur Peace Agreement (DPA). DPA fails to end the fighting.

2007 New peace talks between Khartoum and rebel leaders. Main rebel leaders refuse to attend. Rebels attack African Union (AU) peacekeepers, killing several. Soldiers and Janjaweed respond with attacks on towns.

2011 South Sudan declares independence from Sudan.

2014 Janjaweed, now known in Sudan as Rapid Support Forces, destroy 127 empty villages.

GLOSSARY

Arabization The process of turning a country into a place for Arabs only.

atrocity A wicked, brutal, or cruel act.

barbarity Extreme cruelty.

coalition An alliance of groups for joint action.

coup The violent overthrow of a government by a small group.

desertification The process of land that was not originally desert turning into desert.

dictator One who exercises supreme authority in a country, usually without having been elected to do so.

ethnic Having to do with large groups of people classed according to common racial, national, tribal, religious, linguistic, or cultural origin or background.

extremist A person who promotes extreme political or religious ideas and does not tolerate other views.

guerrilla Describing a small defensive force of irregular soldiers.

Islamization The process of making something Islamic.

Islamist A person who promotes Islamization.

jihad A holy war fought as a religious duty to spread Islam.

manifesto A document that makes public the beliefs and intentions of a group of people.

mosque A place of worship and prayer for Muslims.

Nazi A member of or having to do with the German political party led by Adolf Hitler during World War II.

nomad A person who moves from place to place.

Nuremberg Trials Trials held in Nuremberg, Germany, from 1945 to 1949 to judge leaders of Germany for their actions during World War II.

op-ed A column on a page of special features opposite the editorial page of a newspaper. Short for "opposite editorial."

propaganda Ideas spread whether they are true or not to support a cause or to hurt an opposing cause.

rape The act of using force to make a person have sex.

sheikh An Arab chief or tribal leader.

sordid Extremely unpleasant, filthy, or wretched.

subdue To take control by force of a country or people.

supremacist A person who promotes the false idea that one group of people is superior to others.

visa Permission from government authorities to enter a country.

FOR MORE INFORMATION

Darfur Relief and Documentation Centre (DRDC)
Crêts-de-Pregny 27
1218 Grand-Saconnex
Geneva, Switzerland
Website: http://www.darfurcentre.ch
The DRDC is a nongovernmental organization (NGO) founded in 2004 to work with people from Darfur and other parts of the world to find a way to help Darfur's people end the violence and rebuild their lives. It also maintains a database of groups, researchers, and academics from Darfur.

Darfurian Voices
260 Fifth Avenue, 9th Floor
New York, NY 10001
Website: http://www.24hoursfordarfur.org/contact/
Darfurian Voices seeks to document and broadcast the views of Darfurian refugees on issues of peace, justice, and reconciliation.

Doctors Without Borders
U.S. Headquarters
333 7th Avenue, 2nd Floor
New York, NY 10001-5004
(212) 679-6800
Website: http://www.doctorswithoutborders.org

Doctors Without Borders is a non-governmental organization (NGO) that provides medical aid around the world in response to conflict and natural disasters. It is active in Darfur, and its website provides information about the genocide there.

International Rescue Committee
122 East 42nd Street
New York, NY 10168-1289
(212) 551-3000
Website: http://www.theirc.org
Founded in 1933, the International Rescue Committee is an NGO that serves refugees and communities victimized by oppression or violent conflict worldwide. It is active in Darfur, and its website provides information about the genocide there.

Oxfam Canada
250 City Centre Avenue, Suite 400
Ottawa, ON K1R 6K7
Canada
(613) 237-5236
Website: http://www.oxfam.ca
Oxfam Canada is an NGO that works to end poverty and injustice in countries around the world. It is active in Darfur, and its website includes information about the genocide there.

Save Darfur
1010 Vermont Avenue NW, Suite 1100
Washington, DC 20037
(202) 556-2100
info@savedarfur.org
Website: http://www.savedarfur.org
Save Darfur's mission is to raise public awareness about the situation in Darfur and get people to take action to halt the genocide.

United States Holocaust Memorial Museum
100 Raoul Wallenberg Place SW
Washington, DC 20024-2126
(202) 488-0400
Website: http://www.ushmm.org
The United States Holocaust Memorial Museum is a living memorial to the Holocaust of World War II. Its website provides information about genocide in general and about the genocide in Darfur.

United to End Genocide
1010 Vermont Avenue NW, Suite 1100
Washington DC, 20005
(202) 556-2100
info@endgenocide.org
Website: http://endgenocide.org
United to End Genocide is founded on the work of the Save Darfur Coalition, the Genocide Intervention Network, and

the Sudan Divestment Task Force. It is devoted to educating people about genocide and what they can do to stop it. It also provides information on fund-raising and events around the country.

WEBSITES

Because of the changing nature of Internet links, Rosen Publishing has developed an online list of websites related to the subject of this book. This site is updated regularly. Please use this link to access the list:
http://www.rosenlinks.com/BWGE/darfur

FOR FURTHER READING

Burlingame, Jeff. *The Lost Boys of Sudan*. New York, NY: Marshall Cavendish Benchmark, 2012. Ebook.

Cooper, John. *Raphael Lemkin and the Struggle for the Genocide Convention*. New York, NY: Palgrave Macmillan, 2015.

Des Chenes, Elizabeth, ed. *Genocide*. Farmington Hills, MI: Greenhaven Press, 2007.

Disco, James et al. *Echoes of the Lost Boys of Sudan*. Dallas, TX: Brown Books Publishing Group, 2011.

Friedman, Mark D. *Genocide* (Hot Topics). Chicago, IL: Heinemann Library, 2012.

Gifford, Clive, et al. *Refugees*. London, England: Belitha Press Ltd., 2002.

Hecht, Joan. *The Journey of the Lost Boys*. Rev ed. Jacksonville, FL: Allswell Press, 2006.

January, Brendan. *Genocide: Modern Crimes Against Humanity*. Rev. ed. Brookfield, CT: Twenty-First Century Books, 2014. Ebook.

Kavanaugh, Dorothy. *Sudan and Southern Sudan (The Evolution of Africa's Major Nations)*. Broomall, PA: Mason Crest Publishers, 2014.

Perl, Lila. *Genocide*. New York, NY: Cavendish Square, 2011.

Springer, Jane. *Genocide*. Toronto, ON, Canada: Groundwood Books, 2006.

Xavier, John. *Darfur: African Genocide*. New York, NY: Rosen Publishing Group, 2007.

BIBLIOGRAPHY

Assyrian International News Agency. "Amid Escalating Fear of Massacres, Assyrians Commemorate Martyr's Day." Retrieved September 23, 2007 (http://www.aina.org/releases/20040807203428.htm).

The Avalon Project at Yale Law School. "Nuremberg Trial Proceedings, Vol. 1, Indictment: Count Three." Retrieved October 4, 2007 (http://www.yale.edu/lawweb/avalon/imt/proc/count3.htm).

BBC News. "Rwanda: How the Genocide Happened." Retrieved September 22, 2007 (http://news.bbc.co.uk/2/hi/africa/1288230.stm).

Berenbaum, Michael. "Holocaust." *World Book Multimedia Encyclopedia*. Chicago, IL: World Book, Inc., 2001.

Britannica Online Encyclopedia. "Crusades: The Albigensian Crusade." Retrieved September 19, 2007 (http://www.britannica.com/eb/article-235535/Crusades).

Britannica Online Encyclopedia. "Genocide." Retrieved September 19, 2007 (http://www.britannica.com/eb/article-9036419/genocide#283846.hook).

Britannica Online Encyclopedia. "International Criminal Court." Retrieved September 19, 2007 (http://www.britannica.com/eb/article-9390314/International-Criminal-Court#786622.hook).

Cheadle, Don, and John Prendergast. *Not on Our Watch*. New York, NY: Hyperion, 2007.

Commission for Historical Clarification. "Guatemala: Memory of Silence." *Report of the Commission for Historical Clarification: Conclusions and Recommendations.* Retrieved September 22, 2007 (http://shr.aaas.org/guatemala/ceh/report/english/toc.html).

Daly, M. W. *Darfur's Sorrow: A History of Destruction and Genocide.* New York, NY: Cambridge University Press, 2007.

EuropaWorld. "Raphael Lemkin." Retrieved September 19, 2007 (http://www.europaworld.org/issue40/raphaellemkin22601.htm).

Flint, Julie, and Alex de Waal. *Darfur: A Short History of a Long War.* London, England: Zed Books Ltd., 2005.

Gavin, Philip. "Genocide in the 20th Century: Armenians in Turkey, 1915–1918." The History Place. Retrieved September 23, 2007 (http://www.historyplace.com/worldhistory/genocide/armenians.htm).

HistoryWorld. "History of the Peloponnesian Wars." Retrieved September 22, 2007 (http://www.historyworld.net/wrldhis/PlainTextHistories.asp?historyid=ac46).

International Crisis Group. "Conflict History: Sudan." Retrieved September 20, 2007 (http://www.crisisgroup.org/home/index.cfm?action=conflict_search&l=1&t=1&c_country=101).

The International Tribunal for the Former Yugoslavia. "Case No. IT-95-5-I: The Prosecutor of the Tribunal Against Radovan Karadzic, Ratko Mladic." Retrieved September 22, 2007 (http://www.un.org/icty/indictment/english/kar-ii950724e.htm).

Kumar, Akshaya. "Darfur, the Genocide America Forgot." Al Jazeera America. April 18, 2014. Retrieved December 16, 2015 (http://america.aljazeera.com/opinions/2014/4/darfur-genocide-unitedstatessudanjanjaweed.html).

Lemarchand, Rene. "Chad." *World Book Multimedia Encyclopedia*. Chicago, IL: World Book, Inc., 2002.

Office of the High Commissioner for Human Rights. "Convention on the Prevention and Punishment of the Crime of Genocide." Retrieved September 19, 2007 (http://www.unhchr.ch/html/menu3/b/p_genoci.htm).

Perkins, Kenneth J. "Sudan." *World Book Multimedia Encyclopedia*. Chicago, IL: World Book, Inc., 2001.

Pham, J. Peter. "REM: Islamist Terrorist Regime in Khartoum." *World Defense Review*, June 1, 2006. Retrieved October 26, 2007 (http://www.defenddemocracy.org/in_the_media/in_the_media_show.htm?doc_id=375101).

Pranger, Robert J. "Genocide." *World Book Multimedia Encyclopedia*. Chicago, IL: World Book, Inc., 2001.

Prevent Genocide International. "Ongoing Actions." Retrieved September 19, 2007 (http://www.preventgenocide.org).

Rummer, R. J. "Genocide." Genocide: Meaning and Definition. Retrieved September 19, 2007 (http://www.hawaii.edu/powerkills/GENOCIDE.ENCY.HTM).

SaveDarfur.org. "We Are United to End Genocide." Retrieved December 16, 2015 (http://savedarfur.org/).

Security Council. "South Sudan Conflict Could Unravel Darfur Peace Attempts, Efforts to Normalize Ties with Sudan, Peacekeeping Chief Tells Security Council." United Nations.

January 23, 2014. Retrieved December 16, 2015 (http://www.un.org/press/en/2014/sc11260.doc.htm).

Steidle, Brian, and Gretchen Steidle Wallace. *The Devil Came on Horseback*. New York, NY: PublicAffairs, 2007.

Sudan Tribune. "ICC Prosecutor Pleads Again with UNSC to Act on Darfur Suspects." December 15, 2015. Retrieved December 16, 2015 (http://www.sudantribune.com/spip.php?article57385).

United Human Rights Council. "Cambodia Genocide (Pol Pot)." Retrieved October 4, 2007 (http://www.unitedhumanrights.org/Genocide/pol_pot.htm).

Ward, Dan Sewell. "The Albigensian Crusade." Library of Halexandria. Retrieved September 19, 2007 (http://www.halexandria.org/dward220.htm).

Washington Post. "Sudan in Crisis." 2006. Retrieved December 16, 2015 (http://www.washingtonpost.com/wp-srv/world/interactives/sudan/).

World Without Genocide. "Darfur Genocide." 2015. Retrieved December 16, 2015 (http://worldwithoutgenocide.org/genocides-and-conflicts/darfur-genocide).

INDEX

ABOUT THE AUTHOR

Zoe Lowery is an avid student of history, constantly reading and studying about the past and other thought-provoking topics. She has written and edited a number of books on the topic for Rosen Publishing. Lowery lives in Colorado.

Janey Levy is an editor and author who lives in Colden, New York. She has written more than seventy-five books for young people. She regularly supports the work of the International Rescue Committee and Doctors Without Borders, two of the major organizations helping Darfur's refugees and IDPs.

PHOTO CREDITS

Cover (photo) Education Images/Universal Images Group/Getty Images; cover (cracked texture) Marbury/Shutterstock.com; p. 5 John D McHugh/AFP/Getty Images; p. 7 © Image Bank/Alamy Stock Photo; p. 10 Photo 12/Universal Images Group/Getty Images; p. 13 Roland Neveu/LightRocket/Getty Images; p. 15 © iStockphoto.com/pawel gaul; p. 17 Paul Popper/Popperfoto/Getty Images; p. 19 MCT/Tribune News Service/Getty Images; p. 21 Carolyn Cole/Los Angeles Times/Getty Images; p. 24 Salah Omar/AFP/Getty Images; pp. 27, 34 Scott Nelson/Getty Images; p. 30 Khaled Desouki/AFP/Getty Images; p. 31 © AP Images; p. 36 Ashraf Shazly/AFP/Getty Images; p. 37 Barry Iverson/The LIFE Images Collection/Getty Images; p. 41 Craig Barritt/Getty Images Entertainment/Getty Images; p. 43 Majority World/Universal Images Group/Getty Images; p. 44 Getty Images; p. 47 Anadolu Agency/Getty Images; back cover, pp. 8, 9, 12, 21, 22, 23, 29, 33, 43, 46 (skulls) rangizzz/Shutterstock.com; pp. 7, 15, 24, 31, 39 (top) pimchawee/Shutterstock.com; additional background textures Reinhold Leitner/ Shutterstock.com, © iStockphoto.com/ShutterWorx

Designer; Brian Garvey; Photo Researcher: Heather Moore Niver